Thoughts….At arms length

(A Collection of Poems)

By

Pat McCann

~~~~~~~~~~~~~~~~

First Printing: 2015

ISBN 978-1-326-32198- 7

Pat McCann

Dublin

Ireland

Contents

~~~~~~~~~~~~~~~

Foreword
By Shane Ross.

This is a courageous work by Pat McCann.
Courageous, because he is publishing his first book of
poems at the mature age of 73.
Courageous, because he simultaneously tackles the
varied subjects of Romance, Nature, Dublin, Life and
Spirituality.

Pat has drawn on his experiences of a life well -lived to
create a compendium of carefully crafted poems that
would put some of the more fashionable current crop of
amateur poets to shame.

He has won several awards for his poem 'Hope' from
the Poetry Forum in the UK, a real recognition of the
work he has put into his poetry in recent years.   My own
favourite "Did Ya Ever?" should be read in a broad
Dublin accent. Try it. Or alternatively, ask Dublin
/Ballinteer man Pat, reared in the Liberties, to read it to
you. He did it for me and it sounds wonderful.

Happy reading

Shane Ross

<u>Life</u>

Bridge Across my Dreams

Hope

I Sang my Song

Lonely in a Crowded Room

Dreams

Out of Step

Outside Reality

Posterity

Once Upon a Dream

~~~~~~~~~~~~~~~

Bridge Across My Dreams.

Sometimes a bridge to pleasure,
Of laughter, love and sighs.
Yet still a bridge of yearning,
Filled with sadness, tears and cries

Transit now to my desire;
Then again to my disdain.
Through the blue and sunny skies,
Or dark clouds filled with rain.

Over streams and lakes and rivers
To a land that knows no care.
Where there is no room for gloom
And peace is reigning there.

With close of eyes at eventide
My spirit wanders free.
Across the bridges of my dreams,
That lead myself to me.

Pat McCann

HOPE

So twisted, lies the road of life
And dark clouds shed their tears.
Though futile seems this journey
Strewn with doubt and pain and fears.

Yet now, not time for lingering
Mid the turmoil or the pain.
Seek out the silver lining,
And cause hope to shine again.

For eyes, that are cast downward
Cannot see the road ahead.
Nor love be shown to others,
From a heart that's filled with dread.

Perseverance in the effort,
Though it seems so hard to cope;
Brings inner spirit comfort,
A true harbinger of hope.

Despite the road still bending,
Under skies that look forlorn.
Hope will see you reach your goal,
To a bright and sunlit dawn.

Pat McCann

I Sang my Song

I sang my song unto the world,
I sang it loud and clear,
But the world it kept revolving
And no-one stopped to hear.

I sang my song to innocence,
No guilt, no fault, no shame.
In childish style exuberance,
Without a trace of blame.

I sang my song to justice,
Equality for all.
The rich kept getting richer,
While the poorest took the fall.

I sang my song to freedom,
Defending nations plight.
Too many flag draped heroes
In caskets, cant be right.

I sang my song to finance;
Investors, stocks and shares.
Gambling to grow rich it seemed,
Produced its share of cares.

I sang my song to nature.
The mountains and the trees,
Exalted by the oceans roar,
And whisper of the breeze.

As I approach my destiny,
In Heaven high above.
To Him, the way, the truth, the life
I sing my song of love.

Pat McCann

Lonely in a Crowded Room

The crystal ball revolving,
Reflects a lustrous glow
On noisy, rousing revellers
Rejoicing down below.

Hail fellow well met, is the call,
In voices slurred and loud.
So many sorrows drowning,
As he moves among the crowd.

Surrounded by this happy throng,
Solitarily he stands
And sips a lonely whisky,
While his repertoire he plans.

This Saturday entertainer,
Prepared now for his task,
Swallows down his final dreg,
Once more assumes the mask.

Then stepping up onto the stage
He lifts the microphone,
"Good evening all and welcome."
No longer lonely or alone.

Pat McCann

DREAMS

As we check out from life's daily trudge
And into slumber fall
Letting go each gripe and grudge
Forgiving one and all

On a journey to the land of dreams
A transport so sublime
Through mountains sky and forest streams
Without hindrance from time

In dreams with ease we can achieve
Life's highest aspiration
The fruits of our ambition receive
With no fuss or perspiration

As dreams make things believable
No matter what our aim
In life become achievable
Be it Fortune Love or Fame

Dreams reflect just who we are
Or what we want to be
Like a pointer or a guiding star
They can shape our destiny

Pat McCann

Out of Step

I of the world and in the world
Have marched in step, in time
The world it played its melody
Exquisite and sublime
Never a stumble in the stride
Along the worldly way
I grasped at every chance I passed
But who was left to pay

I of the world and in the world
Now full of introspection
From left to right or right to left
Unsure of my direction
No more the footfall keeping pace
To the cadence of the tune
My flag has reached its time to furl
In life's' late afternoon

Pat McCann

Outside Reality

In Dreams my spirit wanders out
Through the mists of times now o'er
Amid the ghosts of memory
Precious moments to restore
Again I hear the rush of tide
As it echoes childhood days
With cry of terns and squeal of gulls
To a Brass band as it plays

This vision slowly fades away
A young lovers tryst I see
Two hearts are beating now as one
Underneath the cherry tree
Pink petals rained down everywhere
In this cherry blossom dream
With her touch of Springtime madness
Mother Nature ruled supreme

Then my heavy heart forlornly
With deep yearning at its core
Weeps for my forgotten youth
Past and gone for evermore
Sadly like my dream now fading
As my spirit calls me back
Again to stark reality
And life's Winter, cold and black

Pat McCann

Posterity ?

What may be seen in time to come,
Of times that now are here?
Can scribbles on a poet's page
Show life or love or fear?

Will destiny keep register
And words not be in vain?
Their input on the human heart,
Forever to remain.

Or rather just for here and now
Where urgings come to nought?
Perused then simply passed on by,
Not given any thought.

Each line that flows from poet's pen,
Its' story to unfold.
Today's thoughts for tomorrow's times,
By poetry foretold.

Pat McCann

Once Upon a Dream

Those days of expectation,
Sadly, long since passed and gone.
Where life held out its promise
Like the breaking of new dawn.

The road stretched out before us.
Filled with prospects and with hope.
This rising generation,
Held the world within its scope.

But plots and plans can falter,
With eagerness abated.
A thwarting of ambition
As destiny dictated.

No more the road is golden,
Nor success its final theme.
That was once our every wish,
Just once upon a dream.

Pat McCann

Nature

The Acorns Destiny

Aprilesque

Autumn's Glory

Facets of Nature

Hunters Moon

Moonlit Lake

Morning Glory

Night Sky

Nocturnal Tide

Paradise Perhaps

Purple Haze

River of Life

Springing

Sunrise

Where Silence Speaks

~~~~~~~~~~~~~~~~~~~~~

THE ACORN'S DESTINY

Being a bright and balmy day,
I rambled far and free
Stopping awhile for short repose
Underneath an old oak tree

Relaxing there I became aware
Of a gentle soothing sound,
A resonance in harmony
With nature all around

It was the leaves and branches
Swaying to and fro with ease
Marking time in perfect motion
To a symphony of breeze

In company with birds and bees
I was totally as one
In their haven of protection
From the wind and noonday sun

Though rays beat down with midday heat
A sanctuary I had found
While sheltered 'neath its foliage
Pleasant coolness did abound

With gratitude I dallied there
As this thought occurred to me
"To ground did fall, one Acorn small
That became this great Oak tree"

Pat McCann

APRILESQUE.

Reflectively my mind drifts out
where bluebirds play and fly
While Sun and balmy breeze unite
to cause the earth to dry
Where butterflies flit to and fro
as rainbows follow rain
And sunflowers turn their heads in joy
to see the Sun again

At once I hear a rippling brook
where minnows swim and play
In rocky beds by grassy banks
and mounds of loamy clay
I hear the distant Cuckoo cry
seeming oh so far from me
Again it calls, on my ear it falls,
from a close by Maple tree

Upon the breeze there comes the scent
of grass just freshly mown
From a garden lawn that just this morn,
the daisies did adorn
Magnolia , hydrangea, tulips,
all bloom in one accord
While the purest Easter Lilies
 remind us of the Risen Lord

Here nobly stands the Chestnut tree
Its young green leaves on show
Spreading out its far flung branches
as they sway to winds that blow.
I see the apple blossom fall
like snowflakes from the sky
Carpeting all the field around
as on the ground they lie

Heaven opens up its treasure trove ,
Springtime the greatest feature
A gift from God for Man to share
with every living creature
In stressful times we should reflect
on the wonder that is Nature
And say a word of thanks to God
our bountiful Creator .

Pat McCann

Autumn's Glory

Falling leaves yellowed and drifting to ground
Announcing that Autumn is here
And acorns a windfall that squirrels have found
At this harvesting time of the year

Days grow ever shorter as the wind gains in chill
At night harvest moon gives it light
The pumpkins maturing make a pie that will fill
Or a lantern to brighten the night

Out strolling at morning there echoes the crunch
Of the fallen leaves under my boot
Gathered on footpaths where they tend to bunch
In the pond clacks a solitary coot

Come All Saints Eve when lost souls appear
It is said spirits then can be seen
Once known as the start of the Celtic New year
Today it is called Halloween

Fruit now fully ripened by summer's bright Sun
Which too often is taken for granted
Let us humbly give thanks to The Holy One
Who nurtured each seed that was planted

Autumnal dampness now holding its sway
Hoary frost becomes part of the story
Redbreasts twitter at the dawning of day
And Winter dethrones Autumn's glory

Pat McCann

Facets of Nature

Mist enshrouds an evening sky
Until moon and stars take the stage
Barn owls hoot and foxes cry
As nocturnal instincts engage

Somewhere a dawn is breaking
With glory of sunlight aglow
Silently moonlight forsaking
The hills and their valleys below

Sleeping sands are washed awake
Caressed by the slow drifting tide
Rolling pebbles and stones partake
In ebb and flow of waters glide

The wind that blows in o'er the land
Makes soft music through the trees
Corn stalks sway at its command
Collaborating with the breeze

Facets of nature bewitching
With myriad moods on display
Our environment enriching
Through aeons in ordered array

                    Pat McCann

Hunter's Moon

I gazed upon a Hunter's Moon,
Ere the Autumn had its last.
Pale and wan it seemed to me,
With a beauty unsurpassed.
Gleaming thru the evening mist,
It shed its ghostly light.
A portend of approaching chill,
On that still October night.

I gazed upon a Hunter's Moon,
Across the empty distance
And mirrored in its halo there,
Reflections of existence.
Gone is Spring's expectant youth,
No Summer passions yearning.
While leaves surrender to the Fall,
To earth and dust returning.

Pat McCann

MOONLIT LAKE

Passively the ripples lap,
While shoreline they caress
Tho' gently do the breezes blow
The leaves still acquiesce

With faintest hue of aquatic blue
The lake is calm and still
Reflecting brightest moonlight glow
As it rises o'er yon' hill

Overhead a skein of geese
In formation as they fly
To a backdrop of a million stars
That twinkle in the sky

Midges performing Pirouettes
Just above the waterline
Lunar spotlights as they dance
In a ballet oh so fine

The plaintiff sound of curlews cry
Disturbs the peaceful night
Across this liquid mirror so clear
An owl, answers in its flight

Placid water so deep and pure
A tranquility sublime
Is nature's legacy to man
Until the end of time

Pat McCann

Morning's Glory

New dawn breathes life into the world,
As sunrise gives its light.
A chorus of birds sing a welcoming song
And their farewell refrain to the night.

Cock crow calls across valley and plain,
Inviting all sleepers awake.
Announcing the wondrous beauty of morn,
Fading moon looking wan and opaque

Dew laden, latticed cobwebs resemble
A garland with suns golden glaze.
Droplets suspended just above ground
Refract rainbow-like spectral arrays.

Freshening wind rustles leaves in the trees,
Causing branches to dance to its tune.
Shadows foreshorten, as Sun climbs on high.
Morning's glory becoming the noon

Pat McCann.

NIGHT SKY

Twilight arrives in the heavens on high
Night's shadowy canvas preparing
On God's giant blackboard that is the night sky
Widespread clusters of stars are emerging

Glowing quite faintly ere darkness is rife
As it deepens, the brighter they shine
Pulsing and twinkling the sky comes to life
A perfect liaison of Natures design

On the horizon the moon starts to show
Coming up from a curtain of haze
Casting its pale light o'er landscape below
Spectral shadows are cast by its rays

Inky the blueness of background arrayed
With planets and stars to the fore
Brightly the Moon centre stage is displayed
Man and cosmos in perfect rapport

Who but the creator could furnish a scene
As wondrous as this gift of night
A nocturnal vista picturesque and serene
Night sky reigns, until dawn brings its light.

Pat McCann

Nocturnal Tide

With Gentle caress the tide flows o'er the sand
And breaks in a white line of foam
Then with instant retreat makes an exit so grand
Falling back to its oceanic home

The moon in the heavens reflected below
Through calm sea as swift seagulls fly
The blinking and twinkling of stars all aglow
Like lanterns strung out across sky

Again touching shore like a lovers embrace
Harmonising with breeze whispering low
An orchestral performance with ease and with grace
Ebb and Flow, Flow and Ebb, Ebb and Flow

Oh Gentle tide soothing, Oh gentle tide calm
Tide of night and Tide of release
Your rhythmic motions massaging like balm
Bring serenity, comfort and peace.

Pat McCann.

Paradise Perhaps

Beyond the portals of the mind,
There lies a land divine.
Where placid lakes and pastures green
With azure skies combine.
Brightly painted butterflies,
In colourful array.
The rainbow's arch from sky to ground,
A radiant display.
Now birdsong fills the atmosphere
And gentle west wind blows.
Here no-one is an enemy,
Perfect peace forever flows.

Pat McCann

PURPLE HAZE

The azure turns slowly to mauve in its hue,
As the Sun doffs its hat to the sky.
Bidding the darkening heavens adieu,
A lone star in the east shines on high.

Colour enchanting and vibrantly full,
Gloaming's onset, rare beauty displays.
A balm to the spirit as senses they lull.
O'er the scene hangs a deep purple haze.

The mists, adding mystery as dusk starts to fall.
Silent spectres on darkening land.
Deepening shadows mark daylights withdrawal,
Like an ebb tide leaving the sand.

A blackbird perched on a branch so high,
Sings sweetly his evening time praise.
Rejoicing this canvas of heavenly sky,
While deeper, grows God's Purple Haze.

As darkness takes place where twilight has been
And stars set the heavens ablaze.
Enhancing the calm of a nocturnal scene,
Ever fading, the deep purple haze.

Pat McCann

RIVER OF LIFE

Her source in its rising with wonder enthralls
Beginning her childish cascade
Down through the foothills chasing nature she falls
Rills and rivulets join her parade

Ever growing and swelling she glides into romance
With gentility and ease at her leisure
On her dark pools swans glide in ballerina like dance
A performance forever to treasure

Blissfully entering a mystery called love
Where turbulence, or peace can reign
Passion carried as high as the stars up above
Bring excitement and pleasure, or pain

Onwardly tumbling to a space called ambition
With a gushing and troubled flow
Then finds herself calmed, in a place called contrition
Her aquatic head bending low

In the course of this flowing her story she writes
Carving her history through time
Multiplying in volume through days and through nights
A continuum, mundane and sublime

At last at a gateway known as old age
She graciously enters the sea
No longer parading she writes her last page
Becoming collectively free

Pat McCann

Springing

The sun beams through the lattice
And the lark announces morn.
In hedges, fledglings stirring.
A new Spring day is born.

Warm, west winds blowing softly,
Causing daffodils to sway,
The old mill pond to ripple
And falling blooms to play.

Crocus and bluebell scattered
Through their woody domain.
The cuckoo, "Cuc-koo's" his call.
Close by, then distant again.

Streams now swelled by melting snow,
Conjoined with rippling rill.
Mumbling, tumbling as they flow
From high up on the hill.

Out across the meadow land
Where young lambs skip and prance.
Daisies partner dawn's onset
In Nature's Spring-time dance.

Pat McCann

SUNRISE

While easterly gazing
o'er a sea of deep blue.
Stars softly fading
as night bids adieu.
The horizon is tinged
with hint of a glow,
First crimson, then gold
as the sun starts to show.
A refraction of haloes
appear in my sight.
Announcing surrender
of night to the light.
The air fills with birdcall
rejoicing on high
And God's golden gift
takes its place in the sky.

Pat McCann

~~~~~~~~~~

Where Silence Speaks

Silence falls so sweetly on the ear
As dusk is spreading slowly all around
Whispered breezes softly stir the leaves
On branches where they sway above the ground

The softest beams of moonlight from on high
Illuminate the peaceful scene below
Gossamer wispy cloudlets drift on by
Silently and gently as they flow

Upon the air a pleasure so intense
The wafting scent of Jasmine in their bloom
Such fragrance fills the senses to the core
And soothes them with their delicate perfume

In the quiet of the early night alone
Where solitude can set the spirit free
In calm repose I sit beneath the stars
To listen as the silence speaks to me

Pat McCann

Dublin/Nostalgia

Did ya Ever ?

Dublin Homecoming

Dublin Memories

The Salty Man

The Shop Down on the Corner

The Streets Where We Used to Play

Too Many Years

~~~~~~~~~~~~~~~

Did Ya Ever?

Did ya ever scut a horse n' cart when you were just a nip
And hear the other kids call out "scut behind there, Lash the whip"
Or did ya ever bunk into the flix, on a Saturday afternoon
'Til the usher with the big bright torch turfed ya out too bleedin' soon

Have ya ever walked with swingin' arms behind the Sally Army band
As they marched to Portobello bridge, sure the music it was grand
Were ya ever swiped behind the ear with a dishcloth by yer Ma
She'd say go long outta that ya little brat, next time I'll tell yer Da

Did ya ever get chased in Stephens Green just for walkin on the grass
And hide behind the bushes till ya saw the "parky" pass
Did ya ever fish for "Inkers" in the naller near the lough
And bring them home in a jam jar ,havin caught them with yer sock

Did ya ever swing on a scaffold at yer local buildin' site
Until the "Gotchee" chased ya and ya got an awful fright
Did ya ever slip into a crowd at the bus stop for the Zoo
The conductor wouldn't let ya on because ya skipped the bleedin' queue

Well me and my mate Joxer we did all of the above
Our days were filled with fun and Sun and most of all with love
Ahhhh but Dublin towns not quite the same as when we were both eleven
The times so rare no longer there; and Joxers gone to Heaven

Pat McCann

Dublin Homecoming

Me oul' one and me oul' fella,   said "Paddy come sit down
And we'll tell ya of your birthplace, they call it Dublin town
A proud and noble capital, throughout the world renowned
For the craic and Guinness porter, no place like it can be found.

There's nowhere else on earth you'd get, Crubeens served at the bar
Or a 'one and one' like Burdocks do, comin' home after a jar
The pong of Anna Liffey, or the smell of boilin' tar
All remind me of oul' Dublin, Irelands bright and shining star"

Me oul lad he says "Paddy, I remember oh so well
Gettin' on the bus on Sunday, the conductor rang the bell
To take us to the Phoenix Park, Where we'd play and run like hell
We'd be feelin bleedin knackered,when at home asleep we fell."

Me Ma told me about Moore Street, where the traders had their stalls
Selling fruit and veg and fresh fish, she could remember all their calls
Apples, Pears an' ripe bananas , and at Christmas Tinsel Balls
To the strain of carol singers, singing loudly "Deck the halls"

"It was there that you were born lad, but quite soon we had to sail
Across the sea to Holyhead, on the boat that brought the mail
From there by train to Liverpool, where yer Da he got a job
Earned enough each day to pay our way, and to save up a few bob

The people there were good to us, and for nothing did we lack
But both yer Da and me,"she said, "Were always longing to go back,
To our dear and darlin' Dublin, to our family, friends and craic
We both think that time is coming soon our cases we will pack."

So back they went to Dublin but me I stayed behind.
I was working for Royal Liver and me job I had to mind
But I never could stop thinking of me Ma or of me Da
Back in their darlin' Dublin, livin' down near Temple Bar

Very soon I got quite restless and the job I jacked it in.
I travelled cross the Irish Sea to me roots and to me kin.
Back to where I once belonged and here I felt at ease
In a flat I found I settled down in Dublin's Liberties.

Me own kids now are growing up and learning this from me
There's nowhere else on earth quite like this city by the sea
Me Ma and Da again they've moved, this time to Heaven above
But to me they left their Dublin, to be part of and to love.

Pat McCann

DUBLIN MEMORIES   Pat McCann

Aaahh Some things that I remember in days of yesteryore,
Like Peggy's Legs and Acid Drops and bars called Cough No More.
There were Jacobs broken biscuits only tuppence for a bag
And a Woodbine for a ha'penny if ya were gummin' for a drag.

There were characters a plenty of every shape and style.
We had Forty coats, Skin the goat and a bloke called Twister Doyle.
But the best of all was Bang Bang who made a noisy fuss,
Shootin' everyone with his back door key from the platform of a bus.

The kids played games like 'kick the can, 'piggy beds' and 'relieveoh'.
On a rope tied around the lamp-post, they would swing both to and fro.
We rolled marbles down the gully and caught jackstones on our hand
And at Dollymount on sunny days we built castles in the sand.

We had hooleys on a Sunday when the relations came to call.
Carryin' brown bags from the boozer sure we'd have a bleedin' ball.
Me Ma did all the cookin' and me Da would slice the ham.
The older ones had sambos and us kids just bread and jam

Then after tea was over and they took the corkscrews out,
Sure ye'd hear the corks all poppin' from the porter and the stout.
Uncle Christy calls out "Order please cos' Im gonna give yiz a song."
He'd sing "Oh to be in Doonaree" and he'd have the words all wrong.

By the time it got to ten o'clock, nearly everyone was fluthered.
Auntie Molly is wailin' "Danny Boy", like a tom cat that was neutered.
Now its nearly time to head for home, the last bus is half past ten.
But next Sunday in Auntie Molly's house we'll do it all again.

Oh Yes I still remember those days of innocence and fun
And hold them dear within my heart until life's race is run.
Though yesterdays are over and tomorrow no one sees,
I still hark back to the good oul' craic and my Dublin Memories.

THE SALTY MAN

The Salty Man sits at the end of the pier
Atop of an old rusty capstan
Each day he would come here to sit and to stare
The local folk call him "the captain"

His tanned face a road map, etched deeply with lines
From the sea, and the wind, and the spray
His mind a confusion from too many wines
And his hair now a silvery grey

This harbour town was his last port of call
His sea legs now feeble and weak
As his Clipper sailed off from the old harbour wall
He watched; as tears rolled down his cheek

Ne'er again on the briny would The Salty Man roam
With escort of Dolphins or Terns
An Inn near the harbour has become his new home
Still his heart for the ocean it yearns

Each day alone now he sits in this spot
And vacantly looks out to sea
For fate dropped his anchor and this is his lot
The Salty Man ever, land bound he will be.

Pat McCann

The Shop Down On The Corner.

Have you ever sat and reminisced about how things used to be
Before the days of superstores, before shopping was a spree
You didn't swipe yer loyalty card and the assistant knew yer name
There was a kindly word and friendly smile, but today its not the same
What with plastic bags and barcodes and plastic money too
Then to pay for what yer buyin' ya have to join a queue.

To go down to our local shop when I was just a boy
with the list me Ma wrote out for me, it always was a joy
"A half a dozen fresh eggs, and a jar of mixed fruit jam
A stone of new potatoes, and   a quarter pound of ham
Six slices of best cheddar, and a fresh turnover too
A tin of Mansion polish, and a bag of Reckitt's Blue

The assistant ticked them off the list as she added up the bill
That'll be six and ten pence she'd say, while opening the till.
The change was three and tuppence and that tuppence was for me.
To buy myself a bubble gum and sweets called honey bee
But supermarkets aren't friendly like the corner shops before
Just try talking to yer trolley as ya push it to the door

The corner shops in Dublin were a place where all could head
To buy the food for dinner, or just a spool of thread,
And I didn't really matter if yer Da was on the sick
If you didn't have the few bob you could get it all on tick
You wouldn't get such favours in a superstore today
Its cash, credit or debit card, that seems the only way

Today our local corner shop has become a convenience store
It opens late to facilitate, but there's no greeting anymore
No nevermore the wit and wile of a friendly conversation
Nor the smile so grand or a helping hand without any hesitation
But progress has its price to pay, and community is the mourner
Oh how I wish I could still repair, to the shop down on the corner.

Pat McCann

The Streets Where we used to Play.

In memory often I return
to times back in the past.
When life was like a theatre play
and we were in the cast.
Those childhood days and simpler ways,
now seem so far away.
Ahh we took the stage, at an early age.
On the streets where we used to play.

Out on the street with a toy-gun and hat,
Roy Rogers I always would be.
While my oul' mate Joxer became Gabby Hayes,
playing support to me.
We fought off the outlaws and Indians too,
from morning till end of our day,
The wild west came alive, at the age of just five.
On the streets where we used to play.

Some days we were soldiers out fighting a war,
like GIs against Japanese.
One legged pirates next day we'd become,
or Tarzan out swinging on trees.
We each played a role down the yellow brick road, '
'neath skies either sunny or grey
Whatever our part, sure we did it with heart.
On the streets where we used to play.

Now Joxer thought he was Errol Flynn,
with a sword that was made out of wood,
A swashbuckling hero who always would win,
but Joxer he never drew blood.
With the 300 Spartans who fought at the pass, l
ike heroes we stood come what may,
With spear and with shield, we never would yield.
On the streets where we used to play.

Like all good productions its run had to end,
development caused its demise.
The fat cats of   property investment decreed,
that progress meant building high rise.
Very soon the *Corpo said to us, "
We're transferring you away"
And we left Dublin town, as the curtain came down.
On the streets where we used to play.

Pat McCann

~~~~~~~~~~~~~~~~~~~~~~~~~~~

*Dublin Corporation Housing Dept.

Too Many Years

Too many years to sit and wait,
Too many years making do.
Too many years of tempting fate,
Too many *tears* flowing through.

Too many years of living the lie,
Too many years spent desponding.
Too many years no sun in my sky,
Too many *ears* not responding.

Too many years being sad and alone,
Too many years trying to cope.
Too many years of life to bemoan,
Too many *fears* without hope.

How many years can I carry on?
How many years more must I cry?
How many years 'til the cloud disappears
And the sun shines again in my sky?

Pat McCann

Romance

Go Gently

Hopes Eternal Glow

A Lovers Lament

Loves Banquet

Mind-set

My Love Brings

Passion

Smiling Heart

These and More

Your Love

~~~~~~~~~~~~~

Go Gently

When you go, go gently,
As life's fervour ebbs and slows.
When you speak, speak softly
Tell of passion's rampant throes

When all is done remember
How you caused my sun to shine
In the Winter of your leaving
Tell the world how you were mine

When you think, think fondly
Lest the memories might erase
Cling closely to each moment
Tell of lover's warm embrace

When you go, go gently
As tears begin to well
Though deeply dark my sorrow
Tell, my love, go gently tell

Pat McCann

Hope's Eternal Glow. (Sonnet)

I linger in despair and feel the pain,
Of life's lost joy, that numbs an empty heart.
Here never more will love sing its refrain,
That symphony enchanted from the start.
Now sorrow haunts the place where first we kissed,
There passions tidal flow we both did share.
Such ecstasy forever to be missed
And memories the heart cannot declare.
Alone I walk the paths of other days,
With none to share this burden that I hold.
Yet still within, eternal hope might blaze
From silent glowing embers not yet cold.
Return to me; Oh joie de vivre divine,
Refill with love this empty heart of mine.

Pat McCann

A Lovers Lament

However blue the sky may be
Or bright the sun shall shine
A darkness fills this empty heart
Now you're no longer mine

Those rainbows that once filled the air
Have lost their lustrous glaze
And faded like your love for me
Across these lonely days

Yet treasured in my memories
Those times when love was new
And passion burned with deep desire
A love once deep and true

Whatever then may future hold
To mend a heart so scorned
Has fate just dealt its final blow
Forever, to be mourned?

Pat McCann

Loves Banquet

Come my love, come sit alone with me.

Enjoin your heart with mine in rapture rare

To share in all the pleasure love may bring

At the table of desire that we both share.

Bring nought but all your beauty and your charm;

Your hair, your eyes, your lips and gentle smile.

Your whispered words that stir my inner soul,

Your fragrance that my senses doth beguile.

Bring nought but all the graces you possess

To this banquet of unbridled joy divine.

Let our hearts beat with passions set aflame

As in warm embrace our bodies both entwine.

Pat McCann

Mindset

Though memory will choose the times
Of love's sweet dream in thought.
Amid the joys so heaven blest,
Lingers also, times so fraught.
Should ever recall emphasise,
Or sadly bring to mind.
Those difficult and troubled days,
Where love was less than kind.
Remember too the beating heart
Mid loves enduring bliss
When romance tasted so divine
In the pleasure of a kiss
While reminisce, selective be
To bury hurt and pain.
Unlike a corpse, 'twill rise anew
To have its day again.

Pat McCann

My Love Brings Me

The Beauty that sunlight
Reflects in her eyes.
The whispering wind
I hear in her sighs.

The gleam of a dewdrop
Upon her soft lips.
The touch of sheer velvet
From her fingertips.

The joy of her laughter
That brings happiness.
The delicate pleasures
Of her warm caress.

The smile of enchantment
On her face so fair.
The sadness of silence
When she is not there.

Pat McCann

~~~~~~~~~~~~~~~~~~~

Passion

A life enriched with dreams, though not yet spoken.
Such trysts, that only lovers can espouse.
Must then man's fantasy remain mere token,
When thought does naught but serve him to
arouse?

Emotion floods the void of constant yearning;
Such has been the way since time begun.
Enkindling a fire, now fiercely burning;
The heart forever craves that special one.

~~~~~~~~~~~~~~~~~~~~~~~~~

Pat McCann

Smiling Heart

Forever in my heart she will remain
Despite the separation all the while
Through days of sadness, loneliness and pain
The girl who touched my heart and made it smile

Her radiance was brighter than the dawn
With a gentleness of nature to beguile
The whisper of her beauty had me drawn
The girl who touched my heart and made it smile

Though circumstance now keeps us far apart
My love endures and nothing shall defile
She captivated me right from the start
The girl who touched my heart and made it smile

Pat McCann

~~~~~~~~~~~~~~~~~~~~~~~~~

These and More

How many stars illume the night,
When the heavens are aglow?
How radiant, a sunbeams light
Shining on the world below?

How gentle is the evening breeze,
That cools the summer heat?
How soothing is a rolling tide,
As both ebb and flow compete?

How fragrant is a garden rose,
At the zenith of its bloom?
How tender is a lover's glance,
Being shared across a room?

How fragile is the dream of love,
We both nurture from the core?
How much I wish loves gift could be,
All these things and even more.

Pat McCann

Your Love

A treasure worth sharing
With those who need caring
Bring them your love

The old and despairing
Who sit blankly staring
Show them your love

If hunger they're bearing
Poverty ensnaring
Give them your love

So never be sparing
With sharing and caring
And you will know love

Pat McCann

<u>Spiritual.</u>

Always

Beyond the Haze

Heart Filled

My Destination

Into the Stillness

Pondering

Somewhere

The Looking Hill

The Voyage

~~~~~~~~~~~~

Always.

Sometimes we face the world alone,
Life's pain too hard to bear.
With the burden of our troubles,
We need someone to share.

In the depths of deepest doubting,
'Mid dejection or despair.
Turn to the one who loves us most,
In honest simple prayer

Let Him help you with your problems
Through those bleak and lonely days
He said "Until the end of time,
I will be with you always"

(Matt.28:20)

Pat McCann

BEYOND THE HAZE

Somewhere out there, glows the Light
That penetrates your darkest night
Beyond your logic and   your gaze
The Light exists beyond the haze.

The haze creates a barrier wall
That only faith can cause to fall
Belief allows the light break through
Bringing Grace and Peace to you.

Embrace the Light with all your will
Allow its beams your heart to fill
Bathed in Light you soon will see
The haze was just illusionary

The Light is God and God is Love
Given freely, from up above
Just call His name in troubled days
He will gently bring you beyond the Haze.

Pat McCann

HEART FILLED

In our lives there is a yearning,
That this world cant satisfy
An empty lonely heart place
Which our logic will defy

Neither riches or possessions
Can fill this empty void
Despite fame or high achievement
There's a longing deep inside

Bravely though we face life's journey
As onwardly we plod
Deep within our soul we know
Our destination it is God

Let us fill this empty heartspace
With a word of invitation
Allowing love into our hearts
To share with all creation

There is no manmade substitute
To compare in Joy or pleasure
With the precious gift of Gods love
Beyond all human measure

Pat McCann

MY DESTINATION.

It seems only yesterday
I had it all planned
The future ahead
I held in my hand
While friends from the past
would fade in my mind
Both good and bad memories
I could leave them behind
Hard work was the transport
to *my destination*

No stopping for respite
or rest or vacation
Enthusiasm fueled
my ambition along
With persistence and effort
I couldn't go wrong
But the road to success
is not always so straight
There are pitfalls and potholes
that cause deadlines to wait

Yet waiting was such
a blessed disguise
Giving time to reflect,
and to then realise
That success at all cost
was just my proposition
But was it according
to God's disposition?
Looking back I can see
that the blueprint was flawed
Disregarding all others,
I sought my reward
It was love that was needed
in this journey of mine
To reach *my destination*
in God's own good time

Pat McCann

_____

Into the Stillness

Somewhere beyond the heart and mind
A journey toward soul
In stillness softer than a mist
A yielding of control

Here dwells silent serenity
The peace of inner truth
Where age is not a consequence
Dependent on your youth

Internal hopes and dreams become
Refreshed, restored, renewed
Like streams of crystal water
Should the spirit be confused

Come sit in contemplation
Life's purpose to fulfil
Enlightened through the power of love
'Mid the presence of the still

Pat McCann

Pondering

I sat alone a pondering
The depths of my inner soul
Considering and wondering
Who is the one in control?

Is man deciding his destiny?
Or just acting out a part?
That fits with his identity
From a script, but not from heart

Be he priest, painter or poet
Or even laureate to kings
He cannot halt the march of time
That each new tomorrow brings

So futile seemed the way ahead
With all my thoughts and plans
When every step on every road
Was in the Masters hands

In this thought I found some comfort
Though yet I pondered still
Could I walk the walk of life
In accordance with His will

Pat McCann

SOMEWHERE

Somewhere there's a graceful place
Where grows a perfect rose
Somewhere there's a peaceful race
Somewhere trouble never shows

Somewhere there's a rainbows end
That has a crock of gold
Somewhere there's a special friend
Someone you can enfold

Somewhere there's no poverty
No suffering or ills
Somewhere exists a money tree
Somewhere there's no bills

Somewhere there's a teddy bear
That hugs you back at night
Somewhere there is one to care
Someone to share your plight

Somewhere there's a wishing well
Where wishes all come true
Somewhere there's that magic spell
Somewhere there's life anew

Somewhere is just within our reach
If only we would try
Somewhere a paradise for each
Somewhere with God on high

Pat McCann

The Looking Hill.

With anxious steps I climb the looking hill,
Where all the gain and pain from life is clear.
To remember every loving train of thought.
Acknowledge those of hatred, doubt or fear.

Engaging with my conscience to recall,
Each man, each soul, each act or careless word.
All those that felt unkindness at my hand,
Through indifference or argument absurd.

Still also on this hill I must avow,
The memories of the love I've shared and known.
Where guidance and acceptance freely flowed,
With fondness and forgiveness truly shown.

The twisting road of life its truth unfolds,
When viewed in retrospection from above.
Yet no darkening shadow shall remain,
In the bright redeeming light of God's pure love.

Pat McCann

~~~~~~~~~~~~~~~~~~~~~

The Voyage

All sails unfurled, my ship afloat
Upon life's ocean flow
Where winds of fate shall take me
Not yet for me to know
The Plan of the master mariner
As yet to be revealed
I pray God Speed be given me
Though my journey be concealed
Through long warm days and darkest nights
My resolve set with my course
Mid seabird calls and stormy squalls
Faith and courage my resource
Still I wait and pray, for that sweet day
When I land on God's golden shore
Where cares and troubles melt away
Life's long voyage finally o'er

Pat McCann

#0069 - 230217 - C0 - 210/148/4 - PB - DID1764795